Celebrating Hockey's History

The Original 6

DETROIT RED WINGS

Eric Zweig

Crabtree Publishing Company

www.crabtreebooks.com

Celebrating Hockey's History
The Original 6

Author: Eric Zweig,
 Member of the Society for International
 Hockey Research

Editor: Ellen Rodger

Editorial director: Kathy Middleton

Design: Tammy McGarr

Photo research: Tammy McGarr

Proofreader: Wendy Scavuzzo

**Production coordinator and
 Prepress technician:** Tammy McGarr

Print coordinator: Margaret Amy Salter

Photo Credits:
Alamy: Cal Sport Media, p 26
CP Images: p 10
Getty Images: B Bennett, pp 11 (top), 24 (top)
Hockey Hall of Fame: Turofsky, pp 12, 13 (bottom); p 16 (top
 left), 23; James McCarthy, p 18; Doug MacLellan, p 19 (top);
 Matthew Manor, p 19 (bottom); Le Studio du Hockey, pp 20, 21
 (top); Hockey Hall of Fame, p 22
Icon Sportswire: Steven King, p 4; Shelly Castellano, p 14;
 Nick Turchiaro, p 25 (top)
Keystone: © Bildbyran, front cover, title page, p 13 (top);
 © Daniel Stiller, p 25 (bottom)
Superstock: Underwood Photo Archives, p 5
Wikimedia Commons: hockeygods.com, p 6; Heritage
 Auctions, p 7; Alex Goykhman, p 8; Michael Righi, p 9, Ken
 Lund, pp 11 (bottom), 15, 16 (bottom), Library and archives
 Canada, p 17 (top right); TGC-Topps Gum Cards, p 17
 (bottom); Tom Gromak, p 21 (bottom); creative commons,
 pp 27, 28; SaveRivers, p 29 (top right); p 29 (top bkgd)

Library and Archives Canada Cataloguing in Publication

Zweig, Eric, 1963-, author
 Detroit Red Wings / Eric Zweig.

(The original six : celebrating hockey's history)
Includes index.
Issued in print and electronic formats.
ISBN 978-0-7787-3438-3 (hardcover).--
ISBN 978-0-7787-3444-4 (softcover).--
ISBN 978-1-4271-1923-0 (HTML)

 1. Detroit Red Wings (Hockey team)--Juvenile literature.
2. Detroit Red Wings (Hockey team)--History--Juvenile literature.
I. Title.

GV848.D4Z84 2017   j796.962'640977434   C2017-903479-0
                                              C2017-903480-4

Library of Congress Cataloging-in-Publication Data

Names: Zweig, Eric, 1963- author.
Title: Detroit Red Wings / Eric Zweig.
Description: New York : Crabtree Publishing Company, [2018] |
 Series: The Original Six: Celebrating hockey's history | Includes index.
 | Audience: Ages: 10-14. | Audience: Grades: 7 to 8.
Identifiers: LCCN 2017029654 (print) | LCCN 2017034425 (ebook) |
 ISBN 9781427119230 (Electronic HTML) |
 ISBN 9780778734383 (Reinforced library binding) |
 ISBN 9780778734444 (Paperback)
Subjects: LCSH: Detroit Red Wings (Hockey team)--History--Juvenile
 literature. | National Hockey League--History--Juvenile literature. |
 Hockey--History--Juvenile literature.
Classification: LCC GV848.D47 (ebook) |
 LCC GV848.D47 Z94 2018 (print) | DDC 796.962/640977434--dc23
LC record available at https://lccn.loc.gov/2017029654

Crabtree Publishing Company

www.crabtreebooks.com   1-800-387-7650

Printed in the USA/102017/CG20170907

Published in Canada
Crabtree Publishing
616 Welland Ave.
St. Catharines, Ontario
L2M 5V6

Published in the United States
Crabtree Publishing
PMB 59051
350 Fifth Avenue, 59th Floor
New York, New York 10118

Published in the United Kingdom
Crabtree Publishing
Maritime House
Basin Road North, Hove
BN41 1WR

Published in Australia
Crabtree Publishing
3 Charles Street
Coburg North
VIC, 3058

Table of Contents

Celebrating
Hockey's
History

The
Original
6

HOCKEYTOWN U.S.A.

Detroit isn't the first city to call itself Hockeytown. It won't be the last, either. Still, it's a pretty fitting nickname. It's not just because the Red Wings have more Stanley Cup wins than any other American NHL team. It's also because the Detroit area has become a **hotbed** of youth hockey.

Minors to Majors

In many American states, high school hockey is the highest level for young players. There's plenty of high school hockey in Michigan too, but the Detroit area is also home to some of the very best minor hockey programs for boys and girls. If you play minor hockey in Canada—especially in southern Ontario—there's a good chance you might play in a tournament against Detroit teams such as Little Caesars, Compuware, Belle Tire, or HoneyBaked.

Detroit was originally awarded an NHL franchise on **May 15, 1926**. Official approval was given at an NHL meeting on **September 25, 1926**.

"The first NHL game in Detroit was played on November 22, 1927. The original Ottawa Senators won 2-1 that night."

In the Beginning

Still, there wasn't much of a hockey tradition in Detroit when its NHL story began. The team, originally known as the Cougars, then as the Falcons, even had to play its home games during its first season of 1926–27 across the border in Windsor, Ontario. There was no rink ready in Detroit yet! Detroit lost that first game 2-0 to the Boston Bruins on November 18, 1926. Success was slow at first, but things started to get better before the 1932–33 season. James Norris bought the team. He changed the name to Red Wings and made sure that coach and general manager Jack Adams had enough money to run the team properly. A year later, Detroit reached the Stanley Cup Finals for the first time. They won the cup in 1936 and 1937 and were a strong team throughout the 1940s.

Top Team

By the start of the 1950s, the Red Wings were the best team in hockey. Led by players such as Gordie Howe, Ted Lindsay, Red Kelly, and Terry Sawchuk, Detroit finished first overall in the NHL standings for seven straight years from 1948 through 1955. They also won the Stanley Cup four times. Still, it would be 42 years before Detroit won its next Stanley Cup in 1997, when players such as Steve Yzerman and Nicklas Lidstrom helped build a modern **dynasty**.

Detroit Red Wings vs Toronto Maple Leafs, 1961

THE NHL AT 100

From a low of three teams in its early days to the 31 teams of today, the NHL has changed a lot in 100 years. Players today are stronger and faster than they've ever been, but there are plenty of oldtimers who'll tell you that the league was at its very best in the days of the "Original Six."

Detroit Cougars, 1926-27

Well, Not Quite Original

Not all of the NHL's Original Six teams are actually original. After the NHL was formed at meetings held in Montreal on November 22 and November 26, 1917, only four teams began play that first season. The Montreal Wanderers dropped out after only a few weeks, leaving the Montreal Canadiens, the Toronto Arenas, and the original Ottawa Senators as the league's only three teams.

Hard Times

The NHL grew to 10 teams during the 1920s, but then came the tough economic times of the **Great Depression** in the 1930s. Teams began to fold. By the start of the 1942–43 season, the NHL was down to six teams: the Toronto Maple Leafs, Montreal Canadiens, Boston Bruins, New York Rangers, Chicago Blackhawks, and Detroit Red Wings. These were the only teams in the NHL for 25 seasons, until the league began to expand again in 1967. That's why they're often referred to as "The Original Six."

Pre-expansion Stars

With so few teams in the NHL, only the very best players made it up from the minor leagues. About 100 players had steady jobs in the NHL in those days, so fans got to know them well. Stars such as Montreal's Maurice Richard and Detroit's Gordie Howe dominated the scoring sheet and still rank high among the legends of the game. Montreal, Detroit, and Toronto **dominated** the Stanley Cup in those days. Between them, they combined to win it 24 times in 25 seasons! Chicago won the cup in 1961, but Boston and New York never won it at all.

Games per Season

50 games in 1942-43

60 games in 1946-47

70 games in 1949-50

During the Original Six era, the length of the NHL season grew from 50 games in 1942-43 to 60 games in 1946-47, then to 70 games in 1949-50. Every team played against the others 14 times each during the 70-game seasons. The top four teams in the standings made it to the playoffs.

Detroit Red Wings, 1952

THE STANLEY CUP

Original Bowl

Who's on First?

The first Stanley Cup champions in 1893 were the Montreal Hockey Club from the Montreal Amateur Athletic Association. But the first players' names were not engraved on the cup until 1907.

Only NHL teams have competed for the Stanley Cup since the 1926–27 season. The last non-NHL team to win the cup was the 1925–26 Victoria Cougars of the Western Hockey League.

WE ARE THE CHAMPIONS

The Red Wings' first Stanley Cup win in 1936 came just six months after the Detroit Tigers won the 1935 World Series and four months after the Detroit Lions won the 1935 NFL championships. Shortly after winning the cup again in 1937, boxer Joe Louis, who grew up in Detroit, became the world heavyweight boxing champion.

Marguerite Norris was the first woman to have her name engraved on the Stanley Cup. She was president of the Red Wings from 1952 to 1955.

More Than a Cup

Donated in 1892 by the then-governor general (the Queen's representative as **head of state**) of Canada, Sir Frederick Arthur Stanley. It was originally just a silver bowl. It has been added to over time and now consists of a bowl plus three tiered bands, a collar, and five uniform "barrel" bands.

Two in a Row

Wings defenseman Vladimir Konstantinov's name appears on the cup twice, for Detroit's 1996–97 win and in 1997–98. Konstantinov was in a car accident in June 1997 and suffered serious head injuries and **paralysis** that ended his career. The Wings still considered him a part of the team, even though he didn't play in the 1997–98 season. When they won the cup again that year, Konstantinov was wheeled onto the ice for a victory lap with the cup. The team also insisted that his name be engraved on it with the rest of the players that year—a move that required NHL approval.

Height: 35 1/4 inches (89.5 cm)

Weight: 34 1/2 pounds (15.5 kg)

By the Numbers

4 goals in one game in a series final was the NHL record set by Ted Lindsay in the 1955 playoffs.

24 appearances in Stanley Cup Finals since 1926 make Detroit's record second only to Montreal's 33.

25 years of consecutive playoff appearances for the Red Wings ended with the 2016-17 season.

42 years of waiting Red Wings fans endured from their team's 1955 Stanley Cup victory over the Canadians until 1997, when they took the cup against the Philadelphia Flyers.

The Red Wings and the Montreal Maroons played the longest playoff game in NHL history on March 24, 1936. Detroit won 1-0 on Mud Bruneteau's goal at 16:30 of the sixth overtime period!

Proving His "Medal"

With his Stanley Cup championship in Detroit in 2008, **Mike Babcock** is the only coach to win the **Stanley Cup**, an Olympic gold medal (2010, 2014), and the **World Championship** (2004). Babcock also coached Canada to a World Junior Championship in 1997. He's now the coach of the Toronto Maple Leafs.

Now Howe About That!

The Howe name has been engraved on the Stanley Cup every time the Red Wings have won it. Syd Howe was a Detroit star for their first three cup wins, but he's no relation to Gordie Howe, who won the cup four times in the 1950s. Gordie's son Marty Howe got his name on the cup as a Red Wings scout for the four most recent cup wins.

Red Wings Winning Years

1936 over Toronto Maple Leafs
1937 over New York Rangers
1943 over Boston Bruins
1950 over New York Rangers
1952 over Montreal Canadiens
1954 over Montreal Canadiens
1955 over Montreal Canadiens
1997 over Philadelphia Flyers
1998 over Washington Capitals
2002 over Carolina Hurricanes
2008 over Pittsburgh Penguins

OOPS!

When Detroit won the Stanley Cup in 1952, coach **Tommy Ivan's** name was engraved as **NIVAN**. **Alex Delvecchio** was spelled **BELVECCHIO**.

Justin Abdelkader, 2008

9

DOMINANT IN DETROIT

Whenever fans and hockey experts talk about the greatest players in NHL history, a few names are guaranteed to come up. Bobby Orr and Wayne Gretzky are popular choices, but both of them agree that the greatest player ever was Gordie Howe.

Gordie the Great

Gordie Howe went to his first NHL training camp with the New York Rangers when he was only 15 years old. A year later, he signed a **contract** with the Detroit Red Wings. Howe began playing professionally in Detroit's **minor league** system when he was only 17, and made his Red Wings debut as an 18-year-old on October 16, 1946. When he played his final NHL game on April 11, 1980, he was 52 years old!

Both Sides Now

Howe played 25 years with the Red Wings from 1946 until 1971 and finished among the top-five scorers in the league 20 times. He won the Art Ross Trophy as NHL scoring leader six times, and the Hart Trophy as MVP six times. Howe was ambidextrous, meaning he could use both hands equally well. He usually shot right, but sometimes switched over to shoot left.

> ## Mr. Hockey
> A player has to be tough to play so long in the NHL, and Gordie Howe was definitely tough. He was very strong, and though he didn't get a lot of penalties, he was never afraid to play a physical game. Sometimes, people called him "Mr. Elbows" but they usually called him "Mr. Hockey."

The Production Line

Early in his career, Howe played right wing on a line with center Sid Abel and left-winger Ted Lindsay. They were the highest-scoring trio in the NHL in the early 1950s and were known as "The Production Line" which was a play on Detroit's status as an auto **manufacturing** city. After retiring in 1971, Howe came back to play for six seasons in the World Hockey Association with his sons Mark and Marty. He then played his final NHL season with his sons as a member of the Hartford Whalers (now the Carolina Hurricanes) in 1979–80.

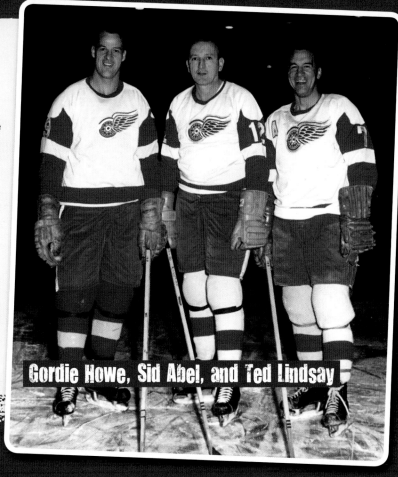

Gordie Howe, Sid Abel, and Ted Lindsay

Howe is the oldest player in NHL history to score **100 points in a single season**. It was two days after his 41st birthday when he hit the 100-point level on March 30, 1969.

In total, Howe played **26 seasons** in the NHL. His lifetime records of **801 goals**, **1,049 assists**, and **1,850 points** were all eventually broken. His regular-season total of **1,767 games** has lasted nearly four decades.

Gordie Howe was the first player in NHL history to score **1,000 points.** He reached the milestone on November 27, 1960.

GORDIE HOWE
"MR. HOCKEY"

GREAT GOALIES

It takes a great goalie for a team to truly become a great hockey team. Back in the 1940s and 1950s, Detroit had so many good goalies that they had to keep trading them away to make room for the next.

Harry Lumley

With many players in their prime serving in the armed forces during World War II, Harry Lumley became the youngest goalie in NHL history during the 1943–44 season. He was just 17 years old. Lumley started the next season in the minors, but was soon in the NHL to stay. He helped Detroit win the Stanley Cup in 1949–50, and though he would make it to the Hockey Hall of Fame one day, the Red Wings traded him away. They knew they had someone even better to take his place.

Terry Sawchuk, who returned to Detroit later in his career, posted 103 shutouts and 447 wins in his 21 NHL seasons. Both were league records that stood for decades before they were broken.

These goalies have played in Stanley Cup-winning championship games for the Red Wings

1936	Normie Smith
1937	Earl Robertson
1943	Johnny Mowers
1950	Harry Lumley*
1952	Terry Sawchuk*
1954	Terry Sawchuk*
1955	Terry Sawchuk*
1997	Mike Vernon
1998	Chris Osgood
2002	Dominik Hasek*
2008	Chris Osgood

* Hockey Hall of Famer

Terry Sawchuk

Terry Sawchuk played his first full season in the NHL in 1950–51. He led the league with 11 **shutouts** and set a new record with 44 wins. Sawchuk won 44 games again in 1951–52. This time, he led the league with 12 shutouts and a 1.90 goals against average. In the playoffs (which were only two rounds in those days) Sawchuk won eight straight games, posting four shutouts and allowing only five goals to lead Detroit to the Stanley Cup. Goalies didn't wear masks at this time, and many of them played a **stand-up style**, trying to keep their faces far away from the puck. Sawchuk liked to play low to the ice, like a modern goalie. It was a lot more dangerous in those days, but Sawchuk felt he could see the puck better that way. He helped Detroit win the Stanley Cup again in 1954 and 1955. Sawchuk would also go on to the Hockey Hall of Fame, but the Red Wings traded him, too.

Glenn Hall

Glenn Hall took over as Detroit's goalie in 1955–56. Like Sawchuk, Hall played in a low crouch, pioneering the "butterfly" style with his pads spread across the ice. Hall only spent two years in Detroit before going on to greater success with Chicago, then St. Louis. Known as "Mr. Goalie," he'd make it to the Hall of Fame, too. Great as he was, Hall never learned how to relax. He got so worked up that he threw up before almost every game.

RED WINGS RECORDS

No less than **28**
Detroit Red Wings players are on the
**NHL's top - 100 greatest
players list.**
That's more than one quarter of the list.
Although several are better known for
their stints on other teams, all donned
the Red Wings uniform for part
of their career.

Record Trouncing
15-0 is the most one-sided score
in NHL history. The Red Wings beat
the New York Rangers 15-0
on February 3, 1944.

Gordie Howe was a First-Team
All-Star 12 times in his Red Wings career, and a
Second-Team All-Star nine times. No one in NHL
history tops his 21 total All-Star selections. Howe
also played in the NHL All-Star Game a record
23 times, including 22 times as a Red Wing.

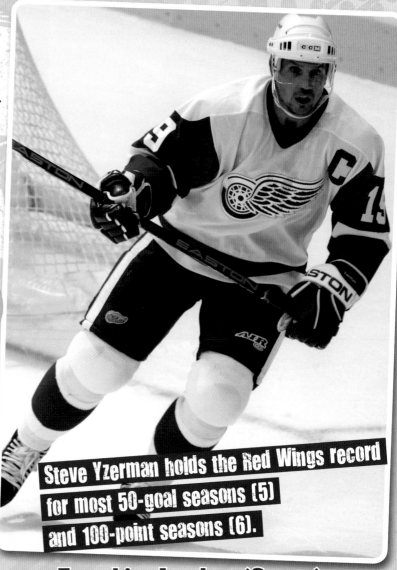

Steve Yzerman holds the Red Wings record
for most 50-goal seasons (5)
and 100-point seasons (6).

Red Wings Regular-Season Franchise Leaders (Career)

Games	Goals	Assists	Points	Wins	Shutouts	Goals-Against Average
1,687	786	1,063	1,809	351	85	1.98
Gordie Howe	Gordie Howe	Steve Yzerman	Gordie Howe	Terry Sawchuk	Terry Sawchuk	Dolly Dolson

Hanging in the Rafters

Only seven numbers have been retired by the Detroit Red Wings, the first being Gordie Howe's No. 9 in 1972. Two more numbers, 6 and 16 worn respectively by Larry Aurie and Vladimir Konstantinov, are "not available" for use.

5	19	12	1	10	7	9
Nicklas Lidstrom	Steve Yzerman	Sid Abel	Terry Sawchuk	Alex Delvecchio	Ted Lindsay	Gordie Howe
(1991–2012)	(1983–2006)	(1938–43, 1945–52)	(1949–55, 1957–64, 1968–69)	(1950–74)	(1944–57, 1964–65)	(1946–71)

 6 goals in one game by Syd Howe on February 3, 1944, is a Red Wings team record.

 7 assists in one game by Billy Taylor on March 16, 1947. This is an NHL record shared by Wayne Gretzky, who did it three times.

 20 years as captain of the team for Steve Yzerman from 1986 to 2006. No other player in NHL history has worn the "C" longer.

 23 straight home wins during the 2011–12 season set an NHL record

 62 wins for the Red Wings to set an NHL record in 1995–96. Detroit went 62–13–7 for 131 points in 82 games, which was one point short of Montreal's NHL record of 132 points set in 1976–77 when they went 60–8–12 during an 80-game season.

Red Wings Franchise Leaders (Season)

Goals	Assists	Points	Wins	Shutouts	Goals-Against Average
65	90	155	44	12	1.37
Steve Yzerman (1988–89)	Steve Yzerman (1988–89)	Steve Yzerman (1988–89)	Terry Sawchuk (1950–51, 1951–52)	Terry Sawchuk (1951–52, 1953–54, 1954–55) Glenn Hall (1955–56)	Dolly Dolson (1928–29)

RED, WHITE, AND WINGED

No NHL team's uniforms have stayed as consistent throughout its team history as the Detroit Red Wings. Even when the team was known as the Cougars and the Falcons, their colors were red and white. The Red Wings logo has remained virtually unchanged since the 1932–33 season.

Reg Noble in a 1930s-era Detroit Falcons sweater

Old D

The first owners of the Detroit Red Wings launched their NHL team in 1926–27 by buying the roster of the Victoria Cougars when the rival Western Hockey League went out of business. Though Detroit kept the Cougars name, the team colors were changed from blue and yellow to red and white. The first Detroit logo was an old-fashioned D, similar to what baseball's Detroit Tigers often wear. The only time that Detroit's NHL team had any other color than red and white was during the two seasons (1930–31 and 1932–32) when the team was known as the Falcons. Red and white were still the main colors, but the team name spelled out on the front of their sweaters and the numbers on the back were in yellow.

Homage to the Auto Industry

In the fall of 1932, James Norris bought the Detroit Falcons. Norris had been trying to buy an NHL team since 1926. He was a wealthy grain merchant from Chicago, but his family had lived in Montreal until he was 18. Detroit was a city known for building cars, so Norris created a new team logo with a wing and a wheel that he based on the logo of the Montreal Amateur Athletic Association. Norris also changed the team's name from Falcons to Red Wings.

Wing-and-wheel logo was based on the Montreal Amateur Athletic Association logo

Elbow Room

It's not clear when hockey players first began wearing elbow pads. It may have been as early as 1910, or as late as 1930. During the 1930s and 1940s, many hockey players wore their elbow pads on the outsides of their sweaters. Some elbow pads even had metal in them, which made them very dangerous to a player getting checked. Metal pads were banned in 1937, but elbow pads and shoulder pads were soon being made of such hard plastic that they became dangerous, too. New rules were passed during the 1950s to say that elbow pads and shoulder pads had to have a soft outer covering. In 1955, a new elbow pad with a soft, rubber cover was developed by Lippman's Tool Shop in Detroit. The Red Wings were the first team to use this new elbow pad.

NORM ULLMAN

DETROIT RED WINGS CENTER

Skilled forechecker Norm Ullman bends a (protected) elbow

TROPHY WINNERS

There's nothing in hockey like winning the Stanley Cup, but here's a look at some Red Wings players who've won the NHL's top individual trophies.

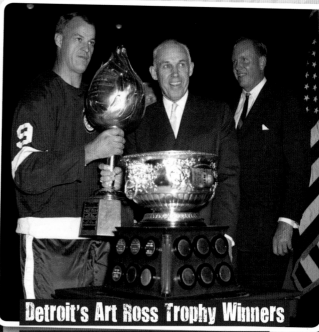

Norris Trophy

After James Norris died on December 4, 1952, his sons and daughter continued to run the Red Wings for another 30 years. Looking for a fitting tribute to their father, the family donated the James Norris Memorial Trophy to the NHL before the start of the 1953–54 season. The Norris Trophy goes to the NHL's best defenseman. Fittingly, the very first winner was Red Wings star Red Kelly.

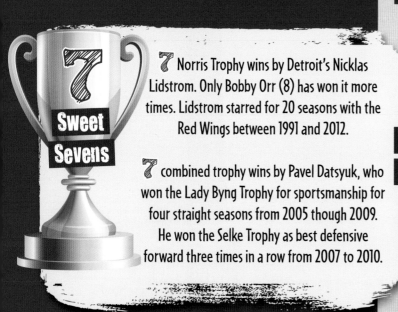

7 Norris Trophy wins by Detroit's Nicklas Lidstrom. Only Bobby Orr (8) has won it more times. Lidstrom starred for 20 seasons with the Red Wings between 1991 and 2012.

7 combined trophy wins by Pavel Datsyuk, who won the Lady Byng Trophy for sportsmanship for four straight seasons from 2005 though 2009. He won the Selke Trophy as best defensive forward three times in a row from 2007 to 2010.

Sweet Sevens

Detroit's Art Ross Trophy Winners (Regular Season Points Leader)

1949–50	Ted Lindsay
1950–51	Gordie Howe
1951–52	Gordie Howe
1952–53	Gordie Howe
1953–54	Gordie Howe
1956–57	Gordie Howe
1962–63	Gordie Howe

Detroit's Hart Trophy Winners (League MVP)

1939–40	Ebbie Goodfellow
1948–49	Sid Abel
1951–52	Gordie Howe
1952–53	Gordie Howe
1956–57	Gordie Howe
1957–58	Gordie Howe
1959–60	Gordie Howe
1962–63	Gordie Howe
1993–94	Sergei Fedorov

Trophies by the Numbers

3 goalies have won the **Vezina Trophy**, including Terry Sawchuk, who won it three times (1951–52, 1952–53, 1954–55). The others are Normie Smith (1936–37) and Johnny Mowers (1942–43).

3 goalies have won the **Calder Trophy** as Rookie of the Year: Terry Sawchuk (1950–51), Glenn Hall (1955–56), Roger Crozier (1964–65).

5 players have won the **Conn Smythe Trophy** as playoff MVP, even though their team didn't win the Stanley Cup. The first was Roger Crozier in 1966 when Detroit lost the Finals to Montreal.

Sweden's Nicklas Lidstrom became the first European-born player to win the Conn Smythe Trophy as playoffs MVP when Detroit won the Stanley Cup in 2002. His teammate and countryman Henrik Zetterberg became the second in 2008.

BEHIND THE BENCH

Two families have owned the Red Wings since 1932. The Norris family owned the team for 50 years until it was bought by Mike and Marian Ilitch, whose family still owns the team today. Some of Detroit's coaches and general managers were with the team a long time, too.

During Detroit's first season in 1926–27, Art Duncan served as the team's captain, coach, and general manager. Teammate Duke Keats took over as coach later in the season.

Detroit Dynasties

Fifty years is a pretty good run by NHL team ownership standards. James E. Norris bought the Detroit Falcons team and their Olympia arena in 1932 and promptly changed the team's name. Norris and his children James D. Bruce, and Marguerite were an NHL dynasty. Along with the Red Wings, James E. was part owner of the Chicago Black Hawks. He was also a majority owner of Madison Square Garden, home of the New York Rangers, and was a financial backer of the Boston Bruins. After his death, the Red Wings were sold to Mike Ilitch. Ilitch also owned the Detroit Tigers baseball team. He died in 2017. His seven children each own a share of the team.

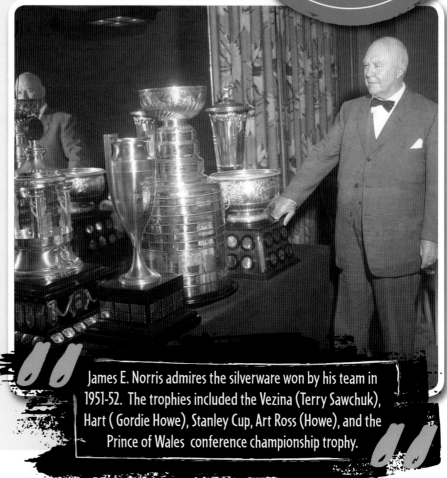

James E. Norris admires the silverware won by his team in 1951-52. The trophies included the Vezina (Terry Sawchuk), Hart (Gordie Howe), Stanley Cup, Art Ross (Howe), and the Prince of Wales conference championship trophy.

Coach Adams

Jack Adams made his NHL debut with Toronto during the league's first season of 1918. He was among the top players in hockey until 1927 when he ended his playing career to become the coach and general manager in Detroit. Adams coached the team until 1947, and was the general manager until 1963. During those years, Detroit won the Stanley Cup seven times. Adams was often called "Jolly Jack," but he wasn't always jolly. He was tough on players when it came to negotiating contracts, and often argued with the referees. Still, he built great teams in Detroit through a strong **farm system** and plenty of trades, which earned him another nickname: "Trader Jack." Adams passed away in 1967. In 1974, the NHL Broadcaster's Association donated the Jack Adams Award to reward the league's coach of the year.

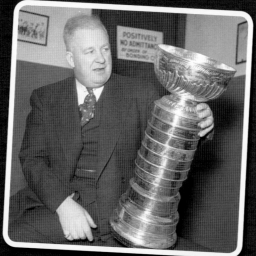

Career Maker

Current Red Wings general manager Ken Holland has a contract through the 2017–18 season that will mark his 35th year with the team. Holland joined the Red Wings as a goalie in 1982, but mostly played in the minors. He joined Detroit's front office in 1985 and has been the team's general manager since 1997. Since then, the Red Wings have won more games than any other NHL team and have won the Stanley Cup three times.

Ken Holland

Red Wings Coaching Leaders

Jack Adams
Seasons 1926-27
Games 964
Records 413 - 390 - 161
Stanley Cups 3

Sid Abel
Seasons 1957-68,
1969-70
Games 811
Records 340 - 339 - 132
Stanley Cups 0

Mike Babcock
Seasons 2005-15
Games 786
Records 458 - 223 - 105
Stanley Cups 1

Scotty Bowman
Seasons 1993-02
Games 701
Records 410 - 193 - 98
Stanley Cups 3

Tommy Ivan
Seasons 1947-54
Games 470
Records 262 - 118 - 90
Stanley Cups 3

RED WINGS BITS AND PIECES

The "Russian Five" were five Red Wings stars who all came from Russia. Coach Scotty Bowman played them together as a unit. They helped Detroit set an NHL record with 62 wins in 1995–96 and win the Stanley Cup in 1997. The Russian Five were defensemen Viacheslav Fetisov and Vladimir Konstantinov, and forwards Igor Larionov, Sergei Fedorov, and Slava Kozlov.

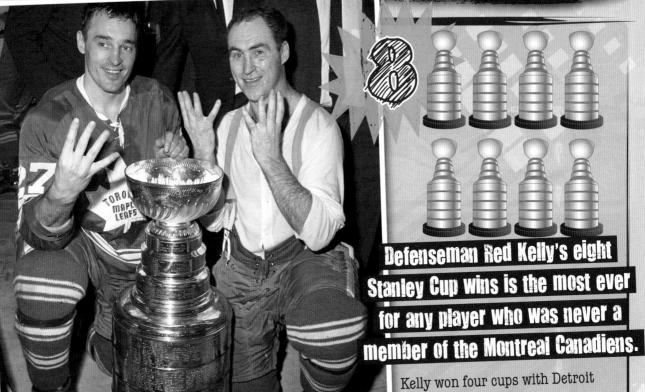

Defenseman Red Kelly's eight Stanley Cup wins is the most ever for any player who was never a member of the Montreal Canadiens.

Kelly won four cups with Detroit during the 1950s and four more with Toronto while playing center in the 1960s.

The Stanley Cup victory for the Toronto Maple Leafs in 1967 was the fourth for star winger Frank Mahovlich. It was the eighth for Kelly who won four with Detroit before joining the Leafs in 1960.

OUCH!

Sid Abel was a longtime player and coach in Detroit. He became known as "Boot Nose" or "Old Bootnose" after he insulted Montreal's Maurice Richard and paid for it with a punch in the face that broke his nose and left it permanently crooked.

Fats wasn't Fat

In his 24 seasons with Detroit, Alex Delvecchio had 456 goals and 1,281 points. Both totals rank third in Red Wings history. Delvecchio was known as "Fats," although he wasn't really fat at all. He just had a very round face.

20 Season Club

In addition to Gordie Howe, who played 25 years in Detroit, three other Red Wings players have also spent 20 seasons or more with the team. Unlike Howe, who played a 26th season with the Hartford Whalers, these players all spent their entire careers in Detroit. They are:

Nicklas Lidstrom	20 seasons;	1,564 games
Alex Delvecchio	24 seasons;	1,549 games
Steve Yzerman	22 seasons;	1,514 games

Nine is the number famously worn by Gordie Howe, but when he began his career back in 1946, Howe was number 17. "We traveled by train back then," Howe once explained, "and guys with higher numbers got the top bunk on the sleeper car. [Switching to] number 9 meant I got a lower berth on the train, which was much nicer than crawling into the top bunk."

Goal, Assist, and Fisticuffs

The term **"Gordie Howe Hat Trick"** refers to a player scoring a goal, getting an assist, and getting in a fight all in one game. Howe was plenty tough and had lots of goals and assists, but never actually got into a lot of fights in his career. He had just two "Gordie Howe Hat Tricks" and both came during the 1953-54 season.

RIVALRIES

During the 1950s, the greatest rivalry in hockey was the Detroit Red Wings versus the Montreal Canadiens. Detroit has also had a long rivalry with the Toronto Maple Leafs, and a short but bitter rivalry with the Colorado Avalanche.

Montreal Match-ups

Although there were only six teams in the NHL at the time, either Detroit or Montreal finished first in the standings every season from 1948 through 1962. During those 14 years, the Canadiens won the Stanley Cup six times and Detroit won it four times. The two teams faced each other in the Finals four times. Detroit won in 1952, 1954, and 1955, and Montreal won in 1956. Those three straight springs from 1954 to 1956 mark the only time in hockey history that two teams have met for the Stanley Cup three years in a row. The Detroit–Montreal rivalry wasn't just about who had the best team, it was also about who had the best player. Canadiens fans worshiped Maurice "Rocket" Richard, who was the game's best goal scorer. But Red Wings fans believed that their own Gordie Howe was the better all-around player. The two were also physical players who clashed on the ice more than once.

In this 1951 game, Detroit's Gordie Howe (#9) and Red Kelly (#4) wrestle for the puck with Canadiens players Dickie Moore (#12) and Maurice Richard (#9).

Red Wings vs Leafs

Over the years, Detroit and Toronto have met in the playoffs 23 times. Only Montreal and Boston, at 34 times, have faced each other more often. Overall, the series is very even, with Toronto winning 12 times to Detroit's 11. When the two teams have met for the Stanley Cup, Toronto holds a clear advantage. The Red Wings won the first time in 1936, but Toronto

went on to win the cup from Detroit in 1942, 1945, 1948, 1949, 1963, and 1964. Since expansion in 1967, Detroit and Toronto have only met in the playoffs three times. The Red Wings won in 1987 and 1988. Detroit was considered a Stanley Cup favorite when they opened the playoffs against Toronto in 1993, but the Maple Leafs upset them with a seven-game victory.

Colorado Avalanche

From 1996 to 2002, Detroit and Colorado were two of the best teams in the NHL. During those seven seasons, the Red Wings won the Stanley Cup three times and the Avalanche won it twice. They were both in the Western Conference then, so they never met in the finals. But they did meet in the playoffs five times, including three series for the Western Conference championship. Colorado beat Detroit in the Western finals in 1996 en route to winning the Stanley Cup. But Detroit beat Colorado in 1997 and 2002, and went on to win the cup both times.

FAN FRENZY

During the years of the NHL's "Original Six," when there were only two rounds in the playoffs, it took only eight wins to secure the Stanley Cup. This led to a strange tradition in Detroit that has been going on ever since.

Origins of the Octopus

During the playoffs in 1952, the Red Wings swept their first round series against the Toronto Maple Leafs in four straight games. Moving on to face the Montreal Canadiens in the Finals, Detroit won the first three games in a row. Heading into Game 4 on April 15, 1952, the Red Wings were one win away from becoming the first team to win the Stanley Cup with eight straight victories. That night, brothers Pete and Jerry Cusimano were going to the game. They owned a seafood store in Detroit and decided to bring an octopus with them. They figured the eight tentacles represented the eight wins needed to claim the cup. So the brothers threw the octopus onto the ice before the game as a good luck charm. The Red Wings beat Montreal 3-0 that night to sweep the series. Fans in Detroit have been throwing the strange-looking sea creatures onto the ice ever since.

After NHL expansion for the 1967–68 season, the playoffs grew to three rounds and it took 12 wins to win the Stanley Cup. There have been four full playoff rounds since the 1981–82 season. Sixteen wins have been needed to take the Stanley Cup since 1987.

Al Sobotka (Detroit Red Wings building manager) swings an octopus over his head in a play stoppage during NHL hockey game.

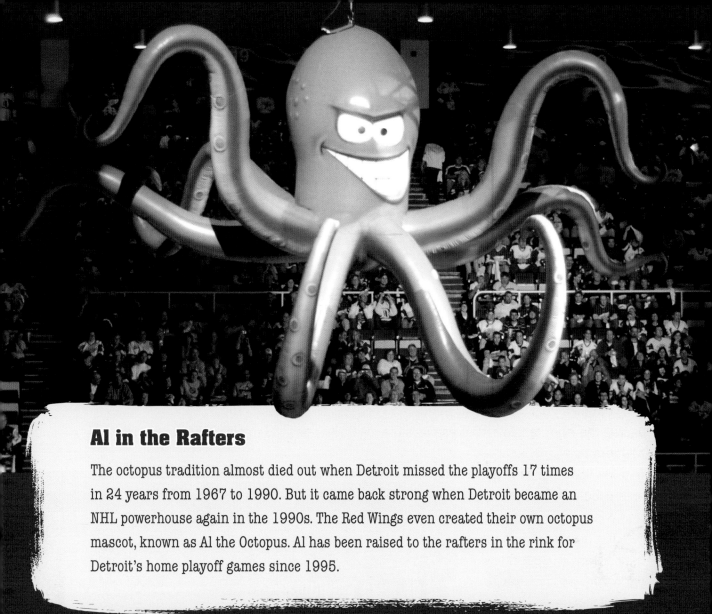

Al in the Rafters

The octopus tradition almost died out when Detroit missed the playoffs 17 times in 24 years from 1967 to 1990. But it came back strong when Detroit became an NHL powerhouse again in the 1990s. The Red Wings even created their own octopus mascot, known as Al the Octopus. Al has been raised to the rafters in the rink for Detroit's home playoff games since 1995.

Florida Copyrats?

Detroit fans aren't the only ones who toss things on the ice. When the Florida Panthers made a surprise run to the Stanley Cup Finals in 1996, their fans threw plastic rats to celebrate goals. The tradition began earlier that season when Panthers player Scott Mellanby used his stick to kill a rat in the dressing room before the game. That night, he scored two goals in the game and his teammates kidded him about scoring a "Rat Trick."

ON HOME ICE

The Red Wings have made their home in four arenas since 1926 and each has a story.

The Border Cities Arena
(Windsor, Ontario)

Built in **1924**, the Border Cities Arena held **6,000 to 9,000 fans**. It was Detroit's first home in the NHL in 1926–27. The "**barn**," as it was nicknamed, was later renamed the Windsor Arena. It was still used for hockey until 2013.

Olympia Stadium

Also known as Detroit Olympia, was home of the Red Wings from 1927 to 1979.

Fun Facts!

- It cost **$2.5 million** to build the Detroit Olympia. That would be equivalent to about **$34.5 million** today.

- Opened with a rodeo on **October 15, 1927**.

- Official capacity was **15,000**.

- The final game was played on **December 15, 1979**. Detroit tied the Quebec Nordiques 4-4. Attendance was **15,609**.

- Also home to the **Detroit Olympics** minor league hockey team in the 1930s and the **Detroit Pistons** of the National Basketball Association (NBA) from 1957 to 1961.

- In addition to hockey, the Olympia hosted many sports over the years, including **boxing, wrestling, and figure skating**. Many concerts and political rallies were also held there.

- The Olympia was torn down in **1987**.

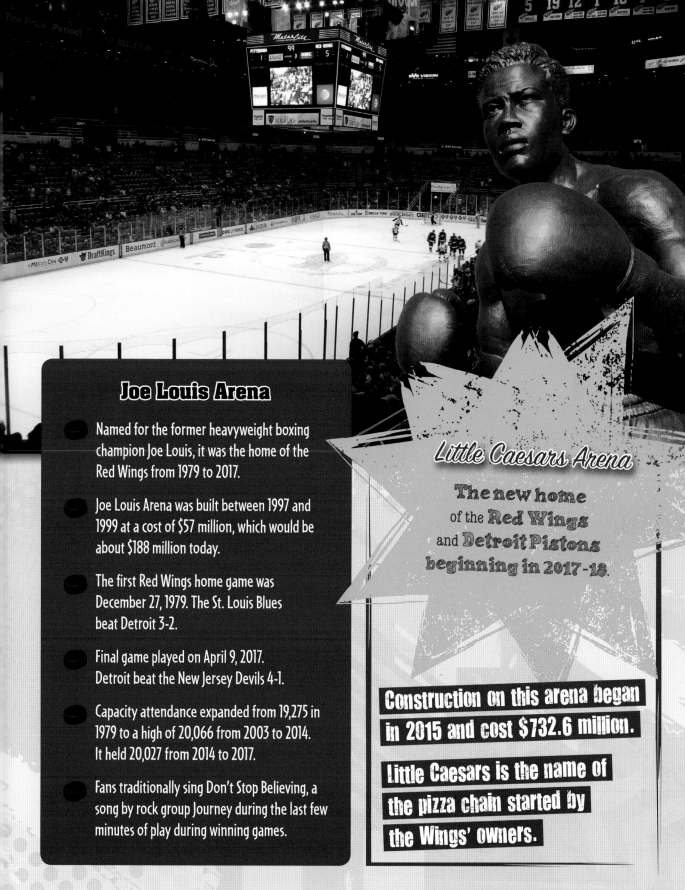

Joe Louis Arena

- Named for the former heavyweight boxing champion Joe Louis, it was the home of the Red Wings from 1979 to 2017.

- Joe Louis Arena was built between 1997 and 1999 at a cost of $57 million, which would be about $188 million today.

- The first Red Wings home game was December 27, 1979. The St. Louis Blues beat Detroit 3-2.

- Final game played on April 9, 2017. Detroit beat the New Jersey Devils 4-1.

- Capacity attendance expanded from 19,275 in 1979 to a high of 20,066 from 2003 to 2014. It held 20,027 from 2014 to 2017.

- Fans traditionally sing Don't Stop Believing, a song by rock group Journey during the last few minutes of play during winning games.

Little Caesars Arena

The new home of the **Red Wings** and **Detroit Pistons** beginning in 2017-18.

Construction on this arena began in 2015 and cost $732.6 million.

Little Caesars is the name of the pizza chain started by the Wings' owners.

29

Glossary

contract An agreement between a player and a team that sets out what each will do, such as play for a certain amount of pay

dominated Ruled over, controlled, or the strongest

dynasty A family or a team that is successful or powerful for a long time

farm system The junior teams where future NHL players learn the skills to play pro hockey

Great Depression A time of worldwide economic crisis from 1929 to 1939 when many people did not have jobs, homes, and money to pay for food

head of state A leader who represents the country such as a queen or king, or governor general

hotbed A place that produces a lot of something, or encourages rapid growth

manufacturing Making something such as cars

minor league A hockey league below the level of the NHL

paralysis The loss of the ability to move a part of the body such as the legs

shutouts Preventing the opposite team from scoring any goals

stand-up style An older style of goaltending, where the goalie plays mostly standing up and rarely drops to their knees to make a save

Further Reading

If you're a fan of the Detroit Red Wings, you may enjoy these books:

The Big Book of Hockey for Kids by Eric Zweig. Scholastic Canada, 2017.

A Hero Named Howe by Mike Leonetti. Scholastic Canada, 2013.

The Ultimate Book of Hockey Trivia for Kids by Eric Zweig. Scholastic Canada, 2015.

Websites to Check Out

The National Hockey League's official website: **www.nhl.com**

The Detroit Red Wings website: **www.nhl.com/redwings**

The Hockey Hall of Fame website: **www.hhof.com**

Hockey Canada's site for kids: **www.hockeycanada.ca/multimedia/kids/**